Nathan Levy's

STORIES WITH HOLES
VOLUME 2
Newly Revised

By Nathan Levy

A collection of original thinking
activities for improving inquiry!

A Nathan Levy Books, LLC
Publication

Nathan Levy Books, LLC
18 Moorland Boulevard
Monroe Township, NJ 08831
Nlevy103@comcast.net
Phone- 732-605-1643
Fax-732-656-7822

ISBN 978-0-9840287-1-9

PREFACE – by Nathan Levy

This book is the result of several years' accumulation of ideas leading to puzzling stories that lend themselves to what I call thinking games. The "games" have become the means for thousands of people to carry on a totally enjoyable process of engaging critical and imaginative thinking. Volume 1 of my Stories with Holes is a collection of stories that has been gathered from various sources. Nathan Levy's Stories with Holes Volumes 2-20 are original. Wherever I speak I share some of the stories with my training groups. Teachers, parents and children enjoy the stories immensely. I hope you will as well.

INTRODUCTION

The objectives of using Nathan Levy's Stories with Holes include the following:

- to provide for growth in imagination and intuitive functioning
- to give experiences that display the fun of working cooperatively, rather than competitively, on a common problem
- to increase cognitive skills of resolving discrepancies through successful experiences
- to provide enjoyable changes-of-pace for task-oriented learning environments

iii

This is a structured activity. It is designed to ensure involvement on the part of each participant, and to promote feelings of group and individual success.

The games are designed to accommodate all levels. "Children" from ages 8-88 will benefit from using these stories.

The time a story takes will vary. Usually a story lasts from 3 to 30 minutes, but some stories can take days. Children, lower grades through high school, tend to regard these thinking games as play instead of work. It is one of the few activities I know of that "hooks" almost anyone into creative use of their intelligence, i.e. learning, almost in spite of themselves. Nathan Levy's Stories with Holes are for all groups over age seven, regardless of background or achievement level.

**Please note that I have revised the above introduction and the following methodology from the way they appeared in the original collection of Stories with Holes. The revisions are based on my current workshop experiences with children and adults.

N.L.

METHODOLOGY

The first time a group plays, it will be necessary to begin by announcing something like the following: "I am going to tell you a story with a hole in it – I mean that an important part of the story is missing. Listen carefully so you can find the missing part, for the story may not seem to make much sense to you at first…"

At this point, tell the story once, pause, and then tell it the same way again. Then say…

"You can ask questions that can be answered either with a "yes" or with a "no". I can only answer "yes", "no", "does not compute", or "is not relevant". If I answer, "does not compute", that means that the question you asked cannot receive a straight "yes" or "no" without throwing you off the track."

Allow for questions about the process, if there are any, but usually it is best simply to jump into the game by having the questioning start. The process becomes clear as the game progresses. Once a group has played the game, the full directions given above for playing the game are unnecessary.

From this point on, answer only in one of the four designated ways. The following is an example of a computed story taken from Stories with Holes, and how it might be played:

v

Story: Mitch lives on the twentieth floor of an apartment building. Every time he leaves, he rides a self-service elevator from the twentieth floor to the street; but every time he returns, he rides the same self-service elevator only to the fifteenth floor, where he leaves the elevator and walks up the remaining five flights of stairs. Repeat, then ask who knows the answer already; if any do, ask them to observe and not give away the answer.

Sample questions participants might ask:
Question: Does the elevator go all the way up?
Answer: Yes.
Q: Does he want the exercise?
A: No.
Q: Does it have something to do with the elevator not working right?
A: No.
Q: Does he have a girlfriend on the 15th floor who he stops to see?
A: No.
Q: Does he have something different about him?
A: Yes.
Q: Is he a robber?
A: No.
Q: Is he a real person?
A: Yes.
Q: A tall person?
A: No.
Q: Is his size important?
A: Yes.
Q: I know! He's too short to reach the button!
A: Right!

At this point, make certain that all the participants understand the answer and why it is the correct answer. In the example given above, the group found the answer quite soon. Instead of starting a new game -- particularly if this is the first time playing – spend some time processing the game with questions like:

* What did you have to do in order to play this game? (Listen, hear each answer, think, imagine, follow a line of reasoning, eliminate possibilities, etc.)

* Ask the person who finally solved the riddle, "Joanne, did you have help from others in finding the answer?" It nearly always comes out that the person relied on previous questions and answers. Use this to point out the interdependence of players, and reduce competition within the group to be the "winner".

* When do you see yourself having to use the kind of thinking you use in this game?

 Usually a group of youngsters will be eager to try a second game right away.

Some important points to remember:

1. Immediately following the telling of each story and before the questioning begins, ask if anyone in the group has heard it before and knows the answer. Tell these people to observe and refrain from questioning.

vii

2. Use the "does not compute" response whenever a single word or phrase in a question makes it impossible to answer with a "yes" or "no" answer. Examples from the story above:

- "Why does he live on the twentieth floor?" "Why" questions, as well as "where, who, when or which", cannot be answered "yes" or "no".

- "Does the elevator operator make him get off at the fifteenth floor?" No mention was made of an operator.

3. If a game goes past 10 or 12 minutes and some people begin to lose interest close the game for the present. There is absolutely nothing harmful in leaving the puzzle unsolved. The group can return to it another time, when interest and energy are high. Some students may protest, but do not give the answer.   The experience of non-closure provides some valuable learning in itself; but more importantly, once a group has expended considerable energy on the game, the victory should be an earned one. Although there may be some unusual circumstances under which you would give the group the answer, I have found it best not to do so (even if some are begging). The point here is not to "take the answer away by giving it." You can always return to it later. What is important is that the students earn the feeling of "we-did-it!"

4. Share the leader role. Once kids have learned how the game works, have a volunteer lead the game. He or

she must choose from the stories he or she already knows. As soon as you are convinced the student is familiar with the story, the answer, and the process (which you should previously have modeled) have the leader read the story to the class and begin taking questions. Most important here is what you model. A child-led game is an excellent small-group activity to have going on while you are occupied elsewhere in the classroom.

5. You may periodically want to encourage categorical thinking. When a player asks a question beginning, "Would it help us to know…" or "Does it have anything to do with…" pause in the game and show how the type of question is uniquely helpful in narrowing down the range of questions, distilling and focusing the group's attention, or cutting away large slices of the topic that are irrelevant. Thus, the question "Is David's occupation important?" tends to be more useful than "Is he a plumber? A teacher?" etc.

6. Be sure that a question is exactly true, or exactly false, before responding. One word can make the difference.

Unique Books Published by
Nathan Levy Books, LLC

A.C.T. 1: Affective Cognitive Thinking
Artistry
Brain Whys
Breakfast for the Brain
Creativity Day-By-Day
Escribiendo Desde El Principio
My Child is Very Special
Nathan Levy's Intriguing Questions – Volumes 1-6
Nathan Levy's Stories with Holes – Volumes 1-21
Nathan Levy's Stories with Holes Gift Sets
Nathan Levy's Test Booklet for Every American
    Over 9 Years Old
Not Just Schoolwork
Perfectionism vs. the Pursuit of Excellence
Principles of Fearless Leadership
Stories With Holes- The Collection
The Trauma Guide: 20 Things Kids with Trauma Wish
    Their Teachers and Parents Knew
There Are Those
Thinking and Writing Activities for the Brain Books 1 & 2
THINKology
True Clues – The African American Whose Clues
What To Do When Your Kid is Smarter Than You
Whose Clues? (History, Music, Literature, Science,
Sports, Authors)
Write from the Beginning

1. The Hissing Sound

The hissing sound led to an investigation. The investigation led to the discovery of drowned parties. The investigator helped prevent future drowning and even greater loss.

Answer:

The hissing sound was a widening leak in a basement pipe. The drowned parties were bugs covered by the leaking water. The discovery of the leak saved the basement from being damaged by the flood.

2. What Sadie Observes

Sadie observes the body. Her report is filed, but not with the police.

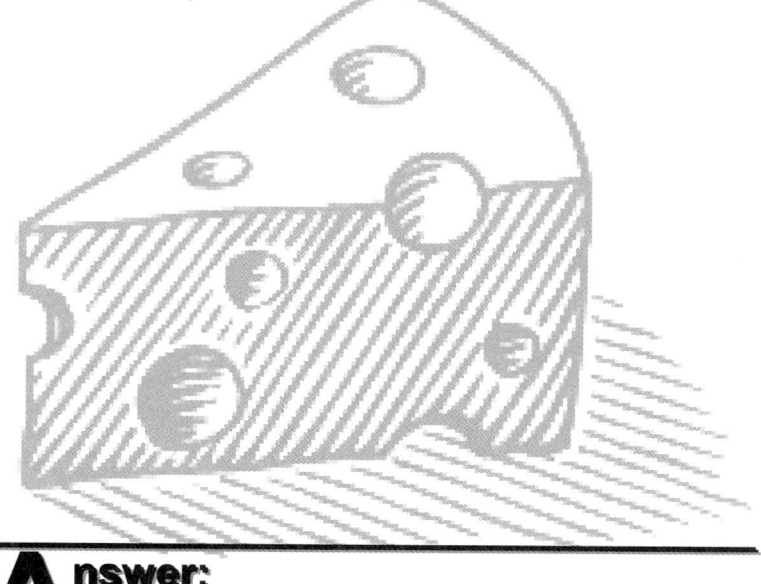

Answer:

Sadie is an astronomer who discovers a new heavenly body through her telescope.

3. He Could Not See

When his eyes were uncovered he still could not see.

Answer:

Mr. Potato's eyes are not for seeing.

4. Cheryl's Piece of Cardboard

Cheryl used the piece of cardboard to get into the large rectangular box. Now in the box, Cheryl observes the results of an activated machine which gives her great pleasure. When the machine is no longer operating, Cheryl throws her remaining cardboard away and leaves the box.

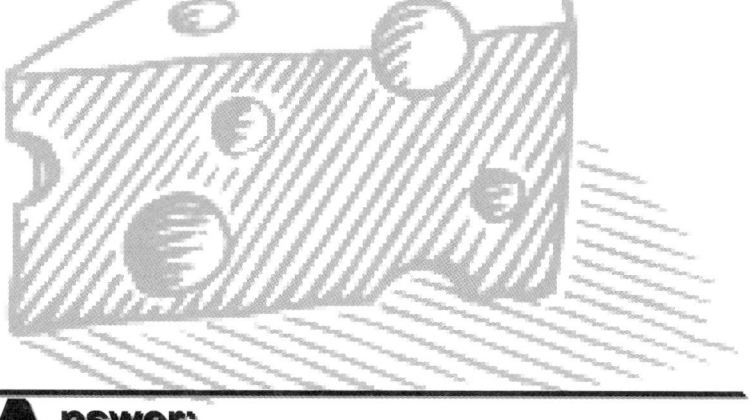

Answer:

Cheryl used a ticket to enter the movie theater. She threw her stub away when the movie ended.

5. The Picnic

The picnic was well attended and very crowded, but no one came to the event.

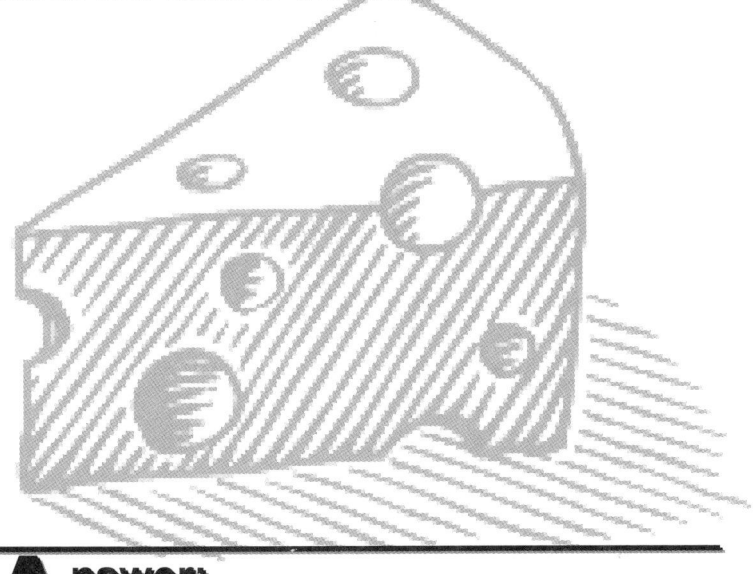

Answer:

The picnic was well attended by crowds of ants and mosquitoes who swarmed around the food which was prepared for people expected to attend. No people showed up.

6. Joanne's Diet

Joanne could eat lobster, but not shrimp. She ate pears, but not apples. Turnips were allowed, but never spinach. Even crab would suffice, but not potatoes, corn or even lamb.

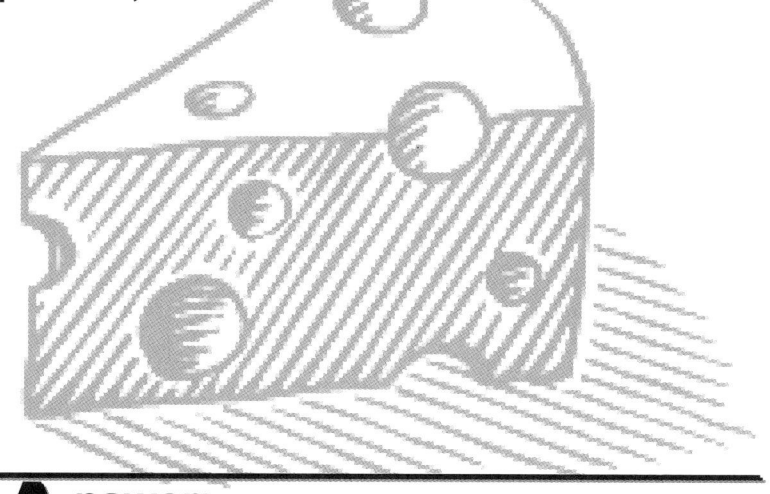

Answer:

Joanne could only eat foods that had at least two letters in the words that are alphabetically ordered (i.e. lob<u>st</u>er, <u>tu</u>rnips, pea<u>rs</u>, cr<u>ab</u>).

7. The Train Accident

Of the 85 people involved in the train accident, all people survived with no major injuries. There were two Dead on the police list.

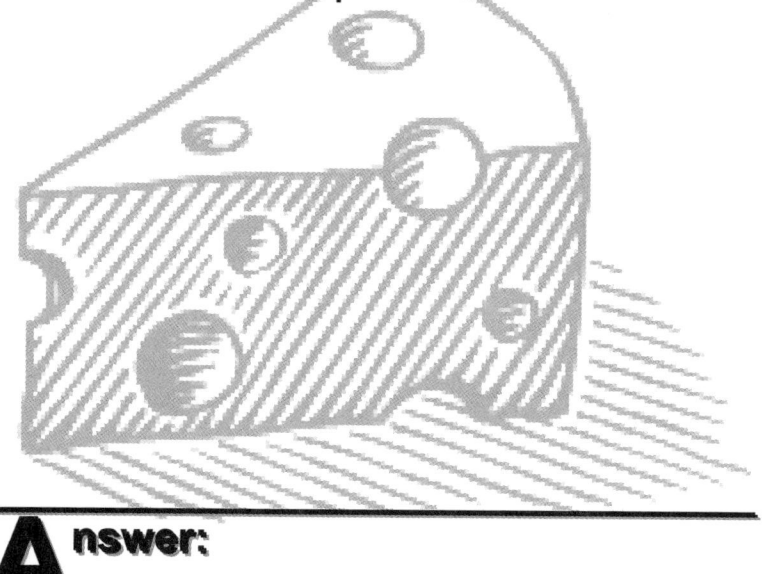

Answer:

Mr. and Mrs. Alan Dead were traveling on the train.

8. Perplexed Detective Cardona

Detective Cardona was feeling lucky and smart! She had deduced clues from the recently discovered hide out of the elusive criminal. A huge wall map was found on the floor with six pin holes clearly visible. Detective Cardona, after two days of examining the map, narrowed her search down to only two locations and traced the criminal to one of them. How?

Answer:

She realized that the four pin holes in the corners were made by the pins holding up the map – leaving only two relatively close locations that had to be searched instead of six in all corners of the world.

9. The Career

Bengy spent his entire career with huge wild animals whose claws and teeth were horribly sharp. Not once was he bitten or clawed by any of the untamed jungle animals. Why?

Answer:

Bengy was a taxidermist.

10. Dr. Mendelowitz's Boast

Dr. Mendelowitz boasted to his fellow surgeons that he does amputations with no pain killers for his patients and no loss of blood. His colleagues had to agree!

Answer:

Dr. Mendelowitz is a tree surgeon.

11. Harry

Harry never uses technology. Harry is a technophobe. Harry miraculously surfs the web as well as anyone. How does Harry do this without help?

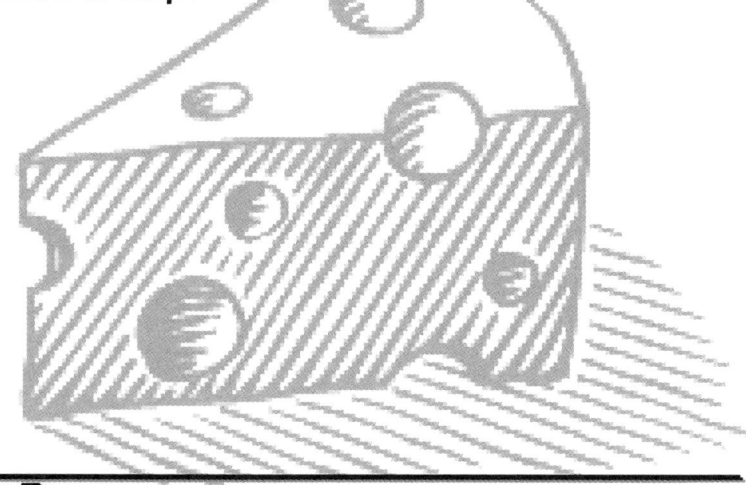

Answer:

Harry is a spider.

12. Carlita's Jump

As Carlita jumped to her death she yelled, "Oh no, I have to do it again."

Answer:

Carlita was being filmed. She knew the scene had not been done right and would have to be filmed again.

13. Odd Numbers

1, 3, 5, 7, 9, 11, 13, 15, 17 and 19 are clearly odd numbers. Joe made two of them even without any mathematical calculations.

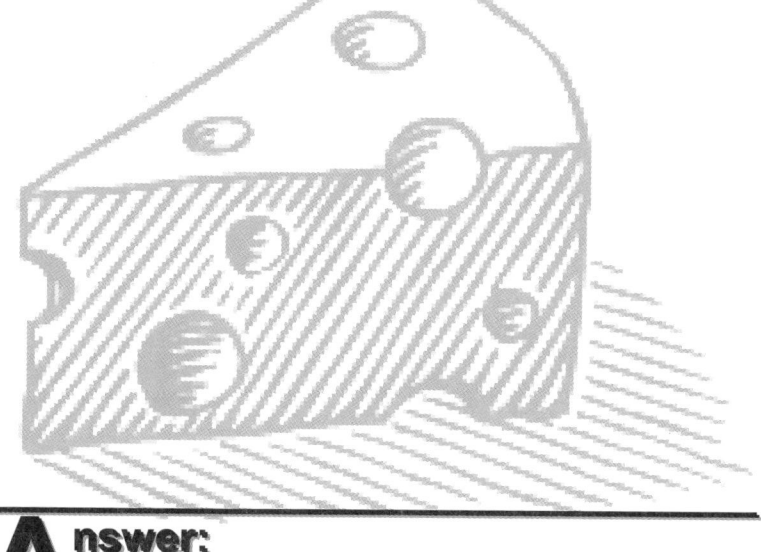

Answer:

Joe took away the letter "s" from "seven" and the "el" from "eleven."

14. The Magic Maguires

The four Maguire girls (Sadie, Nova, Taryn and Joanne) were quadruplets who were claimed to be magical by their mother Marci. Mother Marci's claims were consistently ridiculed on the internet. Marci promised to prove her claims on her daughters' 12th birthdays. As the world watched, Marci displayed proof for all to see. What was the proof?

Answer:

Marci announced that her four daughters would walk on water on their 12th birthdays. Living in Minnesota and being born on January 11, "walking on water" on their 12th birthday was easy for them. The water outside in the frigid winter in Minnesota was hard ice.

15. The Captain's Table

Thirty-five people were seated at the Captain's Table and all felt that they had complete privacy.

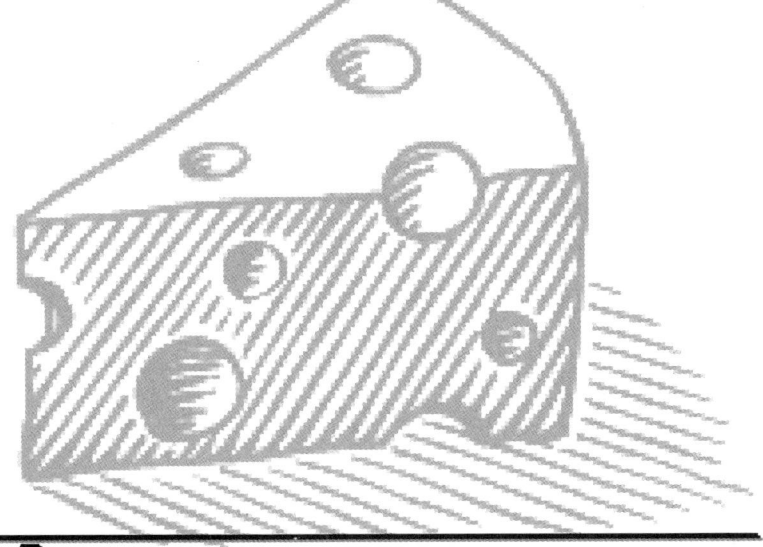

Answer:

The Captain's Table is a restaurant that holds 100 people.

16. The 3 Astronomers

The three astronomers gazed into the evening sky and immediately ran for cover.

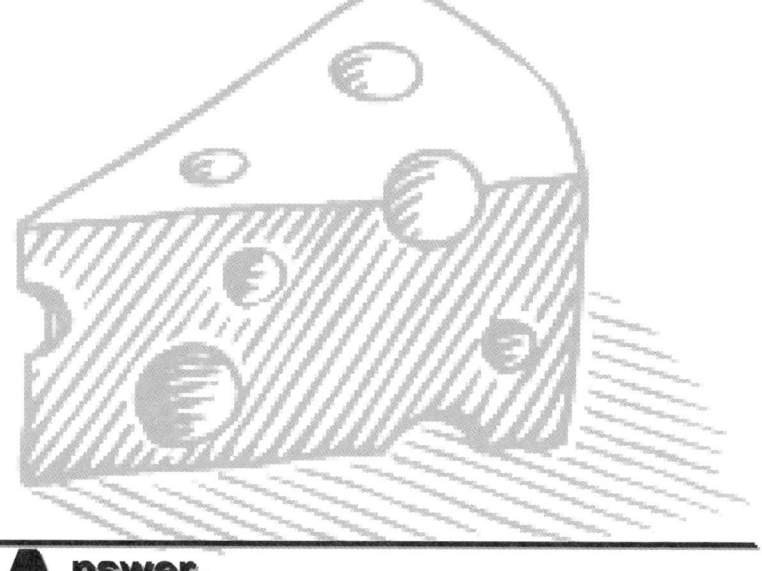

Answer:

They were walking in the street and looked up to see large black clouds – which meant imminent rain. The fact that they were astronomers has nothing to do with the reason they ran for cover.

17. Steph's Boss

"What is the boss like?" asked Steph, the new employee to a friendly co-worker on his first day of work. "When will I meet him? Will I know right away if the boss is nice?"

"You will know before you meet him. Why not call his extension to say hello?"

"I'll do that!" said Steph. He did not need to ask any more questions – nor did he call the boss. Why?

Answer:

The extension for the boss was 666! That told him that the boss was not pleasant due to the devil's extension.

18. Dancing

All of the dancers abruptly stopped dancing.

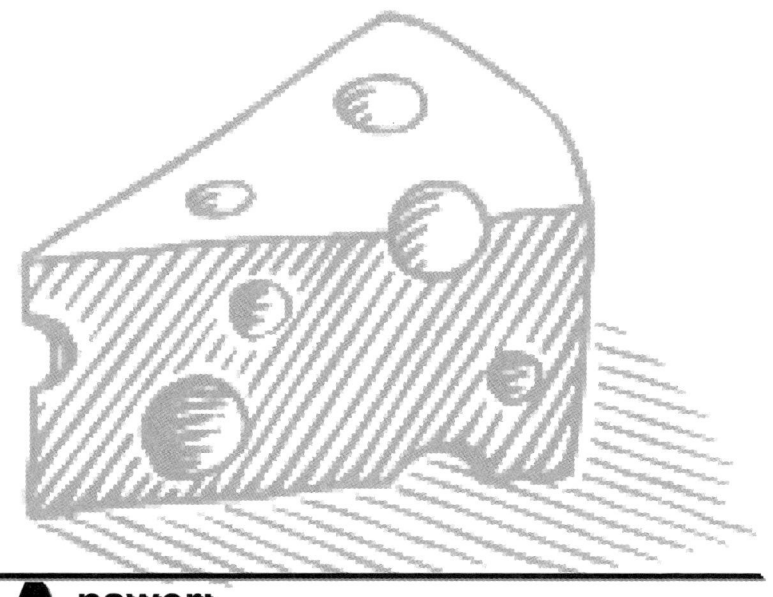

Answer:

The music stopped!

19. The Surgeon's Cut

The surgeon's cut was precise and skillful. It was done after much practice and with approval by the observers. The surgeon paid dearly for what he did.

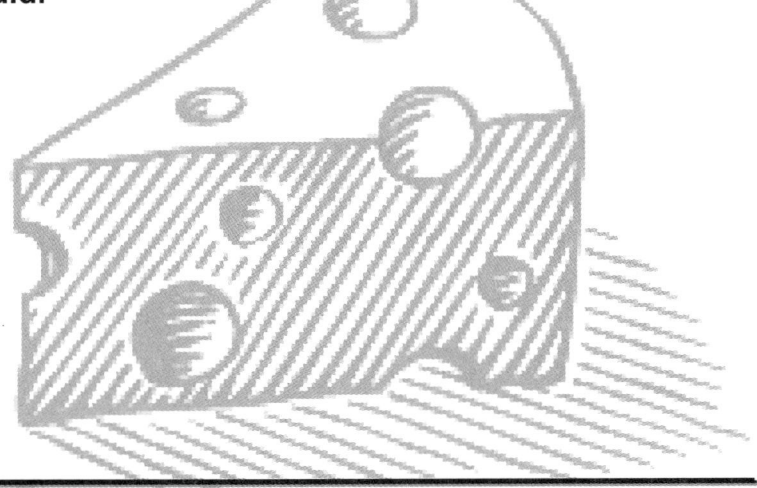

Answer:

The surgeon was playing poker. He cut the cards that were then dealt. He lost a great deal of money on the next few hands – which came out the way they did due to his "cut" of the cards.

20. The Rescuers

The invaders entered through the hole to subdue the guests. Slowly, but surely, the invaders vanquished the guests – much to the host's relief.

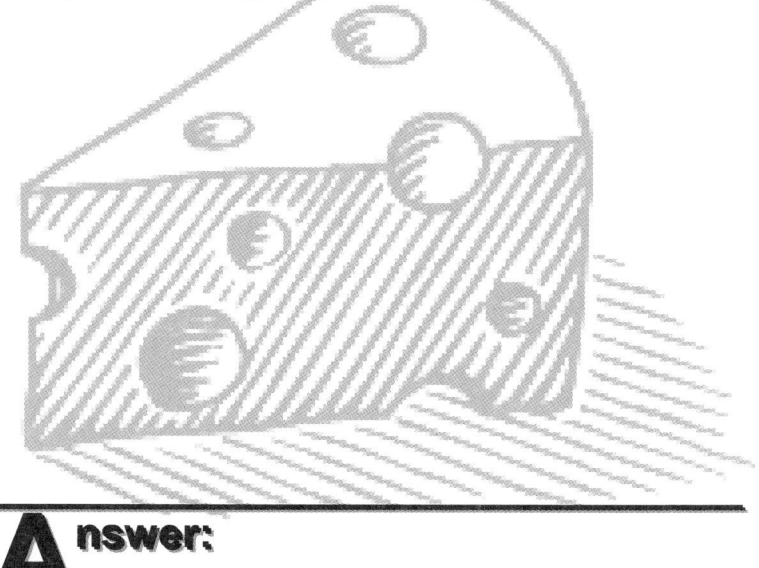

Answer:

The invaders were antibodies injected by needle to take on the germs (guests) being generated by the sickness.

Nathan Levy

Nathan Levy is the author of more than 40 books which have sold almost 250,000 copies to teachers and parents in the US, Europe, Asia, South America, Australia and Africa. His unique Stories with Holes series continues to be proclaimed the most popular activity used in gifted, special education and regular classrooms by hundreds of educators. An extremely popular, dynamic speaker on thinking, writing and differentiation, Nathan is in high demand as a workshop leader in school and business settings. As a former school principal, company president, parent of four daughters and management trainer, Nathan's ability to transfer knowledge and strategies to audiences through humorous, thought provoking stories assures that participants leave with a plethora of new ways to approach their future endeavors.

Nathan Levy Books, LLC is pleased to be the publisher of this book. Teachers, students and other readers are invited to contribute their own "Stories with Holes" for possible inclusion in future volumes. Suggested stories will not be returned to you and will be acknowledged only if selected. Please send your suggestions to:

Nathan Levy Books, LLC
18 Moorland Boulevard
Monroe Township, NJ 08831
Nlevy103@comcast.net
www.storieswithholes.com

Dynamic Speakers
Creative Workshops
Relevant Topics

Nathan Levy, author of the <u>Stories with Holes</u> series and <u>There Are Those</u>, and other nationally known authors and speakers, can help your school or organization achieve positive results with children. We can work with you to provide a complete in-service package or have one of our presenters lead one of several informative and entertaining workshops.

Workshop Topics for School Districts and Businesses Include:

- Helping Children and Adults Become Better Critical Thinkers and Writers
- Practical Activities for Teaching Gifted Children
- Differentiating in the Regular Classroom
- How to Help Children Read, Write and Think Better
- Using <u>Stories with Holes</u> and Other Thinking Activities
- Powerful Strategies to Enhance Learning
- Communicating Better in the Workplace
- How to Teach Hard to Reach Learners
- The Principal as an Educational Leader
  and many more…

Please write or call to receive our current catalog.
Nathan Levy Books, LLC
(732) 605 -1643
NLevy103@comcast.net
<u>**www.storieswithholes.com**</u>